Published in Great Britain in MMXXI by
Book House, an imprint of
The Salariya Book Company Ltd
25 Marlborough Place, Brighton BN1 1UB
www.salariya.com

ISBN: 978-1-913337-79-7

SCRIBO   BOOK HOUSE   SCRIBBLERS

1 3 5 7 9 8 6 4 2

A CIP catalogue record for this book is available
from the British Library.

Printed and bound in Malta.

Author: John Townsend
Illustrator: Rory Walker
Editor: Nick Pierce

Visit
www.salariya.com
for our online catalogue and
free fun stuff.

PAPER FROM

SUSTAINABLE
FORESTS

Interviews with the Ghosts of the

TITANIC

Series created by
David Salariya

Written by
John Townsend

Illustrated by
Rory Walker

BOOK HOUSE
a SALARIYA imprint

Meet the cast

TV crew:

MISH VARMA: HOST OF *LIVE FROM THE CRYPT* TV SHOW

JONTY YARDLEY: CO-HOST OF *LIVE FROM THE CRYPT* TV SHOW

LARNA OBATA: REPORTER

MANDY: HAIR & MAKE-UP

BINTI: DIRECTOR

KEV: CAMERA OPERATOR

ALEEMA: NEWSREADER

DUNCAN: SPECIAL CORRESPONDENT

GAIL FORSE: WEATHER FORECAST PRESENTER

PROFESSOR PUDDLEWORTH: MARITIME HISTORIAN

Ghost Guests:

CAPTAIN EDWARD JOHN SMITH (1850–1912): CAPTAIN OF *TITANIC*

HELEN MELVILLE RUSSELL-COOKE (1898–1973): CAPTAIN SMITH'S DAUGHTER

THOMAS ANDREWS (1873–1912): SHIPBUILDER AND ARCHITECT OF *TITANIC*

ELIZABETH ANDREWS (1910–1973): DAUGHTER OF THOMAS ANDREWS

JOSEPH BRUCE ISMAY (1862–1937): CHAIRMAN OF WHITE STAR LINE AND PASSENGER

MARGARET (MOLLY) BROWN (1867–1932): *TITANIC* FIRST CLASS PASSENGER

JOHN JACOB ASTOR IV (1864–1912): *TITANIC* FIRST CLASS PASSENGER

IDA STRAUS (1849–1912): *TITANIC* FIRST CLASS PASSENGER

BENJAMIN GUGGENHEIM (1865–1912): *TITANIC* FIRST CLASS PASSENGER

VIOLET JESSOP (1887–1971): *TITANIC* STEWARDESS AND NURSE

LILLIAN GERTRUD ASPLUND (1906–2006): *TITANIC* THIRD CLASS PASSENGER

JOSEPH PHILIPPE LEMERCIER LAROCHE (1886–1912): *TITANIC* SECOND CLASS PASSENGER

NOËL LESLIE, COUNTESS OF ROTHES (1878–1956): *TITANIC* FIRST CLASS PASSENGER

SIR ARTHUR HENRY ROSTRON (1869–1940) CAPTAIN OF RMS *CARPATHIA*

Contents

Introduction

Just imagine it... the TV crew arrives on location on board *The Cryptic*, a studio boat with its own submersible vessel. Connected by satellite to crypts around the world, the boat is bobbing on the North Atlantic Ocean, 44 degrees North and 50 degrees West — 2,000 metres (6,562 feet) above the wreck of *Titanic*. Deep down there on the seabed or still inside cabins could be some of the ghosts of those who perished in the famous ship.

These ghosts have never been interviewed on live TV before and the wonders of the latest cutting-edge technology could just make this possible. How could ghosts with dramatic stories to tell refuse the invitation to talk to the team on camera?

What if *The Cryptic*'s deck-manager, tea boy, technicians, make-up team, reporters, presenters and director are all waiting nervously for a 'live encounter with the dead'?

What if we switch on at home for the TV show they said could never be done: *Live from the Crypt*?

Sit back and dare to be stunned...

Stand-by for lights, cameras, music —

ACTION...

Welcome to the programme

MISH:

Hello and welcome to another of our crypt programmes coming to you live...

JONTY:

With a few dead ingredients – in our new series, *Live from the Crypt.*

MISH:

With Jonty Yardley and me, Mish Varma.

JONTY:

Your ghost-hunters searching for some of the most famous ghosts in history.

MISH:

And tonight, we're coming live from the wreck of the *Titanic* in the hope of meeting some of the crew and passengers from the ship's maiden voyage, when she struck an iceberg and sank right here in 1912.

JONTY:

And if we're lucky, we might get an interview with the iceberg.

MISH:

That's silly, Jonty. It would have melted.

JONTY:

Not necessarily. Anyway, maybe icebergs have ghosts. How chilling would that be? If any viewers (or icebergs) have strong views on that question or other issues raised tonight, do tweet or text us.

MISH:

But in the meantime... we probably don't need to remind anyone about the most infamous shipping disaster in recent history. It's a huge story and we're keen to find out from those on board what happened at the moment of impact.

JONTY:

But that's only the tip of the iceberg... as it were. We're here to discover the whole story. What led up to it? Who survived and how? Who was to blame? And the scariest question of all: could it happen again?

MISH:

Not really, Jonty. It's not coming back. *Titanic* has sunk forever.

JONTY:

Ah, you say that Mish – but plans to build a replica ship are shaping up.

MISH:

A shaping ship shortly ship-shape? That's hard to say.

JONTY:

It's a lot harder to do. The original plan was to sail *Titanic 2* by the 110th anniversary year of the original ship, in 2022.

MISH:

What became of the plans, Jonty?

JONTY:

No idea. They've probably sunk without trace. Did you see what I did there?

MISH:

Moving on... although books, plays, movies and musicals about *Titanic* have fascinated the world for over 100 years, no one has yet spoken to the man who was in charge of the ship that fateful night.

JONTY:

That's right, Mish. The *Titanic*'s captain was 62-year-old Edward John Smith. He worked for the White Star Line, which sailed large passenger ships between Britain and the United States of America. Some of those ships were the biggest in the world and the most luxurious for those who travelled first class.

MISH:

Captain Smith, like many of his crew, went down with the ship as it broke up and sank below the freezing waves right here.

JONTY:

I wouldn't like to fall into this ocean. It's very cold, deep and dangerous out there. I hope our boat doesn't hit an iceberg and sink.

MISH:

Navigation equipment today can detect icebergs on the radar so we're fine. Our lifeboat is state of the art, too.

JONTY:

Titanic had twenty big lifeboats, so why didn't Captain Smith just hop into one of those rather than go down with his ship?

MISH:

If you'd done your homework, you'd know all about the lifeboats. Did you watch the famous *Titanic* movie?

JONTY:

No. I know how it ends. Spoiler alert, it sinks. Hmm, that didn't go down well – a bit like the ship.

MISH:

Apparently no bodies have been discovered in the wreck, just watches and shoes. Even bones have dissolved down there. But no one knows what could still be inside enclosed spaces where no fish or crabs can nibble away.

JONTY:

Yuck. Let's just hope we can find some ghosts down there, including Thomas Andrews. He was the ship's architect. He designed *Titanic* to be practically unsinkable. He sank with his ship. I wonder what he's got to say about that.

MISH:

Let's hope we'll soon find out when our on-the-spot reporter arrives at the wreck-site any time now in our special submersible vessel.

JONTY:

Then let's go live to Larna, who is deep below us and hoping to meet the wreck's watery ghosts.

MISH:

And we hope they will want to come up here and join us on our sofa on our floating set in this exclusive *Live from the Crypt* outside broadcast.

JONTY:

Yes, we're connected to several crypts tonight in Britain and America, where our cameras are waiting at the graves of people who didn't go down in the wreck itself. But first, let's see what pictures are coming up from far below us on the seabed.

MISH:

Yes, Jonty – our special cameras and lights are scouring the wreck, as Larna steers the minisub around the *Titanic*'s eerie ballroom and grand staircase...

JONTY:

I can already hear in my earpiece that Larna is sensing a presence. Let's hope it's not a giant squid with an appetite for swallowing minisubs.

MISH:

It's time to be serious, Jonty. We need to stop talking and let Larna see what develops, totally unscripted.

JONTY:

(whispering) So we now join Larna LIVE for 'No script at the ship'. We're gripped!

No Script at the Ship

LARNA:

(*whispering*) Yes, Jonty – I'm down here in the
dark and spooky depths. I am steering around
the promenade deck with its eerily rusty rails and
crusty hull. It's absolutely massive! Now I'm passing
the bridge and peering into Captain Smith's cabin
where I can see a white bathtub and what may be
a desk...

VOICE:

Go away.

LARNA:

I think I heard a voice. I'll extend the ultra-sensitive waterproof microphone and I'll talk into the audio system. Is that Captain Smith, by any chance?

VOICE:

Well, it's not Little Red Riding Hood, is it? What do you want?

LARNA:

We're the team from *Live from the Crypt*, hoping to meet you and Thomas Andrews.

SMITH:

He's around here somewhere. He's always going around with his clipboard to note down all the damage. He can't rest, poor man.

LARNA:

Well, I suppose his great creation didn't live up to its promise, did it?

SMITH:

It was absolutely wonderful – until the last couple of hours. He's been trying to put it right ever since. Anyway, what are you doing down here?

LARNA:

We were hoping you might like to come up and talk to us and maybe meet up with some of the other *Titanic* ghosts. They might join us on the sofa.

SMITH:

Hmph, not if they're just going to complain or ask for their money back. People always want to blame me for the disaster. It really wasn't my fault, you know.

LARNA:

I think viewers would like to know what it was like to be in charge of such an iconic ship and how important you must have been.

SMITH:

Really? Are you sure people don't want to complain that I let them down?

LARNA:

Not at all. Some said you were a hero in keeping cool and helping so many panicking passengers get into lifeboats. Many sang your praises. In fact, for over 100 years there's been an impressive statue of you in Beacon Park in Lichfield that many American visitors visit to pay you their respects.

SMITH:

In that case I may be prepared to come and talk to you... where exactly?

LARNA:

We have a studio boat waiting up on the surface. It's very comfortable.

SMITH:

I shall ask Thomas Andrews to join us. It may take us a while to adjust to fresh air and daylight after being down here for over a century – and we'll take a while to dry out.

LARNA:

Don't worry, we've got towels and a hairdryer. That's amazing – we'll have a world exclusive interview!

So while we wait for you to join us, it's back to Mish and Jonty on the sofa with their fingers firmly crossed...

MISH:

(Back on the sofa) It's sounding promising. And I've just heard we've got other ghost guests on their way.

JONTY:

But we'll put them on ice whilst we're waiting. See what I did there?

MISH:

I think we should try to be respectful, Jonty. No inappropriate jokes.

JONTY:

Good idea, Mish. Then Captain Smith and Thomas Andrews might be keen to spook to us. See what I did there? So, before they join us up here on the *Live from the Crypt* sofa, let's take a look at our plasma screen storyboard to remind us of how the *Titanic* story began...

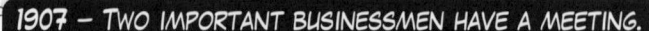

LIVE FROM THE CRYPT

OVER THE NEXT THREE YEARS, *TITANIC* IS BUILT BY HARLAND & WOLFF IN BELFAST.

THAT'S NOTHING. MY AMERICAN CHUM SAYS THAT'S $7,500,000.

IT'S COSTING £1½ MILLION TO BUILD.

SOME OF THE 3,000 BUILDERS ARE INJURED DURING CONSTRUCTION.

Behind the Scenes

BINTI:

There's still no sign of Captain Smith's ghost. We've lost communication with Larna in the sub so I've got no idea what's happening. As the director, I'm in a panic. We won't have a programme if no one shows up anytime soon.

KEV:

The deep-sea camera isn't picking up any images around the wreck.

BINTI:

We'll have to go to a commercial break and get someone to dress up as a ghost. Mandy, as you do hair and make-up, you could easily make yourself look like a drowned mess. You're already halfway there.

MANDY:

(Offended) I've worked hard on this look. Anyway, wouldn't that be wrong?

BINTI:

You're right, Mandy – Kev will have to do it. Give him a grey beard, quick. He can be Captain Smith and you'll have to be a random passenger.

KEV:

I can't talk proper enough to sound like a captain. Anyway, who would work the camera?

BINTI:

I will. No, better still, let's play for time. Bring in that professor of maritime history who navigated us here. Meanwhile, tell Larna to get a move on. Hurry the ghosts!

MANDY:

They'll need some blusher and lippy – or they'll look awful under the lights. They'll look ever so wrinkly after being underwater all that time.

KEV:

Just slap on plenty of powder, Mandy. Yikes, I've just had a signal in my headphones. We've got ten seconds until our sofa goes live around the world.

BINTI:

Quick – Mish and Jonty stand by.

MISH:

What do we say?

KEV:

Seven seconds.

BINTI:

Make something up. Anything. Keep talking until someone shows up.

JONTY:

I can't waffle for long.

MISH:

You usually do.

KEV:

Three seconds... two... one...

MISH:

Welcome back to *Live From the Crypt* where we're anchored above the wreck of the *Titanic*, the final resting place of hundreds of passengers and crew.

JONTY:

And where, any minute now, we will be joined on the sofa by Captain Smith and Thomas Andrews... just as soon as they appear. We hope. Possibly. Perhaps.

MISH:

But in the meantime, we are joined by Professor Puddleworth, who knows all about the *Titanic* and her last days.

PROFESSOR:

(Rushing on) I wasn't expecting this. What do you want to know?

JONTY:

Just give us a few facts and figures about RMS *Titanic*. For a start, what did RMS stand for?

PROFESSOR:

Like other ships in the White Star Line fleet, *Titanic* was a Royal Mail Ship. She was carrying nearly 3,500 sacks of mail, including all sorts of packages.

MISH:

We know the word 'titanic' means 'exceptional strength, size and power', so can you tell us just how big she was?

PROFESSOR:

Colossal. There had never been such a massive ship – almost 300 metres (984 feet) long and nearly 30 metres (98 feet) wide. From the hull to the top of its funnels, she was as tall as a 17-storey building. She was the biggest human-made object ever to move.

JONTY:

All that bulk must have taken a lot of energy to move across the ocean.

PROFESSOR:

You're right. *Titanic* had ten decks, three main engines and its furnaces burnt through about 600 tonnes of coal each day. 175 firemen shovelled the coal by hand and worked in shifts all round the clock. All the boiler rooms made steam to power the engines that drove three enormous propellers. At full speed, the ship could reach 24 knots; that's 43 kilometres per hour (27 mph).

MISH:

That all sounds very hot, steamy, noisy and not very environmentally-friendly.

JONTY:

I don't suppose that bothered the 2,200 people on board for that maiden voyage, Mish. I think I got my numbers right, there.

PROFESSOR:

1,300 passengers and 900 crew. The ship wasn't full and could have held another 1,100 people on board.

JONTY:

She was also the first ever ship to send out an SOS radio signal when things went pear-shaped.

PROFESSOR:

She wasn't. That's an old myth.

JONTY:

Well, ONE of the first. And one of the first to have electric lights, I believe.

PROFESSOR:

Not exactly – but one of the first ships to have a telephone system and electric lights in all bedrooms. That's about 10,000 light bulbs all through the ship.

MISH:

I bet they weren't low-energy lightbulbs, either. I guess she must have dumped tonnes of ash and sewage into the ocean every day.

PROFESSOR:

True. After all, huge amounts of food were eaten on board. When she set sail, *Titanic* carried 1,000 loaves of bread, 36,000 apples and 40,000 eggs.

JONTY:

That would make quite a whopping omelette! Any other little gems to tell us?

I'D BE VERY HAPPY SLEEPING IN SECOND CLASS.

PROFESSOR:

Only that *Titanic* had four elevators, a heated swimming pool, a gym, two libraries and two barber shops. They were for first class passengers, of course.

MISH:

I think there was also a hospital on board.

PROFESSOR:

Yes – on D Deck, at the starboard side close to the second-class dining room and next to the galleys. Handy for those feeling horribly seasick, perhaps.

JONTY:

Seasick? Surely not on a ship that size.

PROFESSOR:

Well, I suppose it didn't bob up and down on the waves like this boat we're on.

JONTY:

Please don't remind me, Professor.

PROFESSOR:

I can feel it all the time sitting here... up and down, up and down, up and down...

JONTY:

Please don't... sorry about this – excuse me *(rushing off)*.

MISH:

In that case, we'd better move on to our next item... whatever it is.

BINTI:

(Through headphones) Go to another plasma screen storyboard or something. Where's Larna? Hurry up with the ghosts – where are they? And will someone get Jonty's head out of that bucket?

KEV:

Cue next storyboard: three, two, one...

STAND BY FOR THE NEXT VIDEO CLIP.

Setting Sail

 BELFAST

3RD APRIL 1912 — *TITANIC* ARRIVES AT SOUTHAMPTON FOR LOADING.

SOUTHAMPTON

CHERBOURG

I'M 24-YEAR-OLD JOHN COFFEY.

YOU CAN BE A STOKER IN THE BOILER ROOM FOR £5 A MONTH.

GALLEY STAFF, FIREMEN, STEWARDS, CLEANERS, ENGINEERS, STOWAWAYS

IN THE FOLLOWING DAYS, THE REMAINING CREW IS RECRUITED...

TITANIC LEAVES CHERBOURG AT 8.10 PM.

TITANIC DROPS ANCHOR IN QUEENSTOWN AT 11.30 AM ON 11TH APRIL, 1912, BEFORE MAIL IS TAKEN ON AND OFF THE SHIP.

Commercial break

Live from the Crypt is brought to you by White Star Line Ocean Cruises, caring for passengers everywhere, whatever their class. Sinkable? Unthinkable!

NEED A BREAK?

KEEN TO TRAVEL?

WANT ADVENTURE?

THEN *TITANIC* ATLANTIC CROSSINGS ARE JUST FOR YOU. ENJOY THE HEIGHTS OF LUXURY AND A FEW SURPRISES ON OUR NEWEST OCEAN LINER. GET AWAY FROM IT ALL AND SAIL WITH US FOR A UNIQUE EXPERIENCE.

OR SIMPLY HOP ON BOARD TO EMIGRATE TO AMERICA WITH ALL THE OTHER COMMONERS.

NEWSREADER:

(Dressed as steward) Welcome aboard. *Titanic*'s interiors are inspired by London's exclusive Ritz Hotel. Relax in our Turkish bath, play squash in our full-size on-board squash court or visit your dog in our luxury kennels. All these are perks of being a first-class passenger. We even have our own on-board newspaper, the Atlantic Daily Bulletin. That always goes down well. In fact, everything on *Titanic* goes down famously well, like no other passenger ship afloat.

Hurry, while prices last. Buy your tickets for *Titanic*'s maiden voyage now.
Prices may vary, terms and conditions apply.

Third-class tickets.........£7 (£800 or $1,000 in today's money)
Second-class tickets...........£13 (nearly £1,500 or $1,900 today)
First-class ticket from.........£30 (over £3,300 or $4,130 today)

First Class with extras (private suites located at the top of the ship, with two large bedrooms, two walk-in wardrobes and a bathroom, as well as a living room for guests):
Full suites cost up to...........£870 (£80,000 or $100,000 today)

BINTI:

(Acting very superior) I am a first-class passenger.
I look down on him.

KEV:

(Acting and trying to sound important) I am a
second-class passenger. I look up to her in first-class.
But I look down to her in third-class.

MANDY:

(Acting very inferior) I am a third-class passenger.
I know my place. I'm not allowed on their deck. I
have to stay with those in steerage class.

BINTI:

Last night we dined in style. The dining room is
the largest ever seen on a ship and a live orchestra
plays whilst we eat eleven courses with champagne.

KEV:

We have a smoking room and a dining room.
Afternoon tea is served in the library.

MANDY:

I know my place. I had rice soup and biscuits
below deck.

BINTI:

Our dining room furniture and panelling is carved
in fine detail in oak, mahogany and sycamore. I
sleep in a four-poster bed, with a private bathroom.

KEV:

My cabin has bunks, a sink and a mirror. Shared bathrooms are available.

MANDY:

I know my place. My cabin sleeps 10 people and is at the noisy bottom part of the ship close to the engines. There are two baths for everyone in third-class.

BINTI:

Entertainment is very civilised. We have a music book containing 352 songs. Musicians on board are required to know them all in case requests are made.

KEV:

Our dining room can seat over 2,000 people at one time and a pianist plays during dinner. The furniture has crimson upholstery.

MANDY:

I don't care. Our meal is basic. 470 passengers eat in three sittings and we make our own entertainment with singing, dancing, smoking and having a good knees-up.

BINTI:

How terribly common. I'm so glad I'm not like him or her!

LIVE FROM THE CRYPT

This is your captain Speaking

EDWARD JOHN SMITH IS BORN IN 1850 IN STAFFORDSHIRE, ENGLAND.

ICE.

ICE.

EDWARD LEAVES SCHOOL AT THE AGE OF 12.

Interviews with the Ghosts of the Titanic

N.B. A LIFEBOAT DRILL, PLANNED FOR APRIL 14TH, IS CANCELLED FOR UNKNOWN REASONS.

Forecast

JONTY:

Whilst we're still waiting for Captain Smith to surface, we can take a look at the weather forecast for *Titanic*'s maiden voyage. So let's go over to Gail Forse. What sort of conditions could *Titanic* expect, Gail? What might be coming their way?

GAIL:

A good question, Jonty. It looks like everything gets off to a good start, with favourable conditions from southern Ireland onwards, as the ship sails south west. Light winds and a few April showers make

for a pleasant stroll on deck, if somewhat fresh and breezy at times. As the wind drops, a little mist and foggy patches may develop in places, but nothing of concern in the navigation room. Although cold, the sea will remain calm throughout.

Late on 13th April, a southerly breeze will pick up but from 6pm the weather will be perfectly clear and fine. The clouds will disappear, the stars will shine and the temperature will drop, so by about 7:30pm the air temperature will be 0.5°C (33°F) and falling to below freezing by midnight. Maybe a little sea ice will drift across the North Atlantic, but there's no doubt that this will be clearly visible from the bridge. So what could possibly go wrong? And that's your forecast.

Sail of the century

JONTY:

Hello again – and whilst we're still waiting for Captain Smith to join us on the sofa, we've managed to link up to a grave in London. Isn't that so, Mish?

MISH:

Indeed, Jonty. Mr Joseph Bruce Ismay, the chairman of The White Star Line that owned *Titanic*, is coming to us live from Putney Cemetery.

JONTY:

Well, almost live. And he's agreed to take part in a quiz that I'm calling 'Sail of the Century'. Sail, as in setting sail, as in ships. See what I did there? After all, the *Titanic* was surely the biggest sailing story from last century. And the man responsible for it all is none other than Mr Ismay.

MISH:

So we now hand you over to Duncan, our quiz master, who will be asking Mr Ismay to sit in the spotlight and score some points. Over to you, Duncan.

DUNCAN:

Yes, welcome to *Titanic Mastermind* and to my guest tonight, known as Bruce Ismay, who masterminded the whole *Titanic* dream. He is about to take his place in the famous black chair... *(Lights lower, music, spotlight on chair)*

ISMAY:

Good evening.

DUNCAN:

You are Joseph Bruce Ismay and what is your occupation?

ISMAY:

Full-time ghost. Former chairman and managing director of the White Star Line.

DUNCAN:

And what is your specialist subject?

ISMAY:

Titanic and me.

DUNCAN:

Mr Ismay, you have one minute to answer the following questions: What job did your father do, Mr Thomas Ismay?

ISMAY:

He was the boss of a shipping company called White Star Line, which he set up.

DUNCAN:

Correct. When did you take over from him?

ISMAY:

When he died in 1899.

DUNCAN:

Correct. In 1907 you met Lord Pirrie of the Harland and Wolff shipyard to discuss White Star's answer to your rival. Who was that?

ISMAY:

The Cunard Steamship Company. We were jealous of their new and very impressive ships – the *Lusitania* and the *Mauretania*.

DUNCAN:

Correct. What was special about your ship, *Titanic*?

ISMAY:

Everything. For a start, her keel had two layers of steel to prevent leaks. She had 16 compartments that could be sealed off using watertight steel doors. If the ship sprung a leak, the doors would close and stop the ship from sinking.

DUNCAN:

Correct, had they worked.

ISMAY:

They did. If two, or even three sections were damaged and water got in, the ship would still have time to sail to safety. Unfortunately, more than three were ripped.

DUNCAN:

So she was sinkable after all, despite your claims that *Titanic* was the 'Ship of Dreams' and the safest ship of all time.

ISMAY:

Well, I may have been a bit wrong about that.

DUNCAN:

Correct. So why did you sail first-class on *Titanic*'s maiden voyage?

ISMAY:

I always sailed on every ship's first trip to check for any teething problems, to keep up the morale of passengers and crew and to enjoy a little luxury.

DUNCAN:

Correct. After all, you also took along with you your valet and secretary.

ISMAY:

Correct.

DUNCAN:

Now I've scored a point! What were the names of your valet and secretary?

ISMAY:

Richard Fry and William Harrison.

DUNCAN:

Correct. What happened to them?

ISMAY:

Pass.

DUNCAN:

I'll accept that answer. They did pass away when they went down with the ship. To be allowed on *Titanic* in the first place, what did passengers need?

ISMAY:

Pass.

DUNCAN:

Correct. When *Titanic* was first tested for safety regulations, what was the result?

ISMAY:

Pass.

DUNCAN:

Correct. Passengers on *Titanic* made music, danced, played cards, sang and entertained each other to make the long evenings what?

ISMAY:

Pass.

DUNCAN:

Correct. When the ship approached an iceberg, it should have steered away and hoped to do what?

ISMAY:

Pass.

DUNCAN:

Correct. Instead, the hull hit underwater ice and ripped open. So how did you get off *Titanic*?

ISMAY:

I stepped into collapsible lifeboat C and escaped.

DUNCAN:

Correct. Apart from the *Titanic*, which was sunk, what else was totally wrecked?

ISMAY:

My reputation. Newspapers called me 'Brute Ismay' for saving myself.

DUNCAN:

Correct. So what happened to you next?

ISMAY:

I resigned not long afterwards. There was a big inquiry and I was blamed for all sorts but I gave a lot of money to the fund for the widows of *Titanic's* crew. I never spoke in public again about *Titanic*. For the next 25 years I lived quietly hidden away in England until I died aged 74.

DUNCAN:

Correct. At the end of that round, Mr Ismay, you have scored 15 points. After that impressive performance, you can now return to rest in peace whilst we visit again the giant plasma screen for the next *Titanic* storyboard...

Collision

14TH APRIL 1912 – CAPTAIN SMITH IS A DINNER GUEST OF MR & MRS WIDENER.

CAPTAIN, THE OYSTERS ARE SLIPPING DOWN FAST!

FAST, INDEED. WE SHOULD REACH NEW YORK IN RECORD TIME.

PSST, YET ANOTHER WARNING OF ICE, SIR.

LET'S HOPE WE DON'T, HA HA.

GOODNIGHT, OFFICER LIGHTOLLER – I'LL LEAVE YOU IN CHARGE.

GOODNIGHT, SIR.

9.20 PM – CAPTAIN SMITH LEAVES THE BRIDGE TO GO TO BED.

In a nutshell

MISH:

Welcome back, whilst we're still waiting for our
ghosts to appear. Apparently it takes a long time for
ghosts to float up to the surface. So we'll go over to
our Special Correspondent who has been given a
real challenge tonight.

JONTY:

Yes, Duncan has the tricky task in *Live from the
Crypt* to make a complicated subject as simple and
short as possible – 'In a Nutshell'.

MISH:

Not only does he have to keep us engaged, but he must also give us the basic facts in under a minute.

JONTY:

And as if that isn't tricky enough, Duncan has just been joined by Professor Puddleworth to explain some big engineering ideas. Over to you, Duncan, and good luck...

DUNCAN:

Yes, welcome to 'In a Nutshell' and a special welcome to Professor Puddleworth.

PROFESSOR:

I'm happy to be back and to explain why the so-called 'unsinkable' sank.

DUNCAN:

I assume the iceberg ripped a huge gash down the entire length of the ship?

PROFESSOR:

Not really, no. True, it punctured *Titanic*'s hull in various places below the waterline, but it was more like a graze rather than a massive tear. Even so, once she began to leak, she began to sink much faster than anyone expected.

DUNCAN:

So maybe you can tell us why the unsinkable quickly became sinkable?

PROFESSOR:

Sure. One reason *Titanic* was sometimes described as unsinkable was because she had a double bottom.

DUNCAN:

Like some people I know!

PROFESSOR:

In other words, her underneath had two layers of steel. The trouble was, she only had a single layer on the sides, which is where she hit the jagged ice.

DUNCAN:

But I thought the designers boasted *Titanic* was divided into many sealed sections so that if one flooded, the rising water wouldn't spill into others?

PROFESSOR:

Ah ha – that was the theory. That worked to a point but the dividing walls, called bulkheads, didn't go high enough. Once she began sinking, water gushed over the top from one section to another. Once a ship starts filling, it tilts and becomes unstable. Then it's only a matter of time.

DUNCAN:

One thing I've never been able to get my head round is how a huge steel ship weighing thousands of tonnes can float in the first place.

PROFESSOR:

Yes, that's a staggering question, isn't it? Of course, it's all down to the design. A ship's body contains an awful lot of air inside. Hold tight for some science now. The ship's shape displaces (pushes aside) enough water so that the buoyancy force is equal to its gravity force. That's why a ship floats. So if a ship weighs 1,000 tonnes, it will sink into the water until it displaces 1,000 tonnes of water.

DUNCAN:

Hmm, I think I followed some of that. So, in a

nutshell, if a ship's hull isn't watertight, water will find its way inside and pull the whole thing down. Gravity will win over buoyancy.

PROFESSOR:

Sure. Just remember, the iceberg scraped *Titanic*'s starboard side underwater. Rivets popped and its steel plates parted from the hull over an 80-metre (262 feet) length. Without a double sidewall, that let in enough water to sink it in just over two and a half hours. That's pretty catastrophic for something that claimed to be extra-safe!

DUNCAN:

Is it true that *Titanic*'s rear – its stern – rose right up out of the water?

PROFESSOR:

Yes, as her bow – the front end – filled right up, it sank first, so the stern lifted clear of the sea. As water rushed into the starboard side of her bow, *Titanic* began to tilt down in front and slightly to the right. By midnight, water in the damaged compartments began to spill over into others because the compartments were watertight only

horizontally and the walls only reached a few metres above the waterline. You can see what I mean on the screen...

DUNCAN:

Your picture doesn't show the stern sticking right up out of the sea.

PROFESSOR:

That happened after about a couple of hours when more water flooded in through anchor-chain holes. As the bow kept sinking, the propellers in the stern were lifted right out of the water. In fact, the stern lifted out of the sea at almost 45 degrees. Because of the tremendous weight of the three large propellers in the stern of the ship, the stresses in the ship's midsection increased so much that the hull split in two. And down she went – the end of the mighty *Titanic*.

DUNCAN:

Thank you, Professor Puddleworth, for explaining all that in a nutshell and within 60 seconds. That gives us enough time to go back to the giant plasma screen storyboard to look at what happened on the stricken *Titanic* within minutes of the iceberg cracking her hull and letting in a great rush of freezing water...

All hands on deck

15TH APRIL 1912, 12.05 A.M.

THINGS AREN'T LOOKING GOOD BELOW DECKS, SIR.

PREPARE THE LIFEBOATS AND GET EVERYONE UP ON DECK.

WE'LL LAUNCH LIFEBOATS AS A PRECAUTION. ALL BEING WELL, THEY'LL ALL BE BACK ON DECK BY BREAKFAST.

THE FIRST FIVE SECTIONS ARE FLOODED. MORE THAN FOUR AND SHE'LL SINK.

SO WHAT'S YOUR ASSESSMENT, MR ANDREWS?

THOMAS ANDREWS DELIVERS NEWS TO CAPTAIN SMITH.

MILLVINA IS ONLY 9 WEEKS OLD.

NUMBER 10 LIFEBOAT IS LAUNCHED.

MILLVINA DEAN WILL BECOME *TITANIC'S* LAST LIVING SURVIVOR, DYING IN 2009 AT THE AGE OF 97.

HELP!

HELP!

MEANWHILE, DOWN IN THE ENGINE ROOMS ALL IS NOT WELL...

How nice to meet you

MISH:

Welcome back to the *Live from the Crypt* sofa with me, Mish Varma...

JONTY:

And me, Jonty Yardley – and we're very excited, aren't we, Mish?

MISH:

Excited and privileged because finally, at last, our special ghost guests tonight have just arrived on set and will be joining us on the sofa any minute now.

JONTY:

Yes, the ghosts of the *Titanic's* captain, Edward Smith, and ship designer, Thomas Andrews, have boarded our boat and are drying themselves off.

MISH:

Yes, the reason we're a little late meeting them is that we've had to bring them up from about two miles below us and put them under the dryer.

JONTY:

Mandy is just helping with a little make-up and brushing them down.

MISH:

Best not do the riddle about the clothes brush, Jonty.

JONTY:

You mean 'what's the difference between a clothes brush and an iceberg?'

MISH:

Not really appropriate, Jonty.

JONTY:

One brushes coats, the other crushes boats.

MISH:

Moving on... welcome Captain Smith and Thomas Andrews.

JONTY:

And the difference between *Titanic*'s designer and an iceberg...

ANDREWS:

Please don't go on about it.

JONTY:

One thinks the unthinkable while the other sinks the unsinkable.

MISH:

Moving on... Let's talk about the triumph that was the magnificent ship, *Titanic*. What was it like for you both to be involved with such a tremendous ship?

CAPTAIN:

She was, indeed, a wonderful ship in so many ways. The trouble is, everyone will always remember her for her disastrous end rather than her glorious start.

JONTY:

Understandable. Is it true there was a nasty fire raging

in one of the coal bunkers for much of the journey?

CAPTAIN:

Nothing to worry about. All under control. These
things happen.

ANDREWS:

It could have weakened a bulkhead and sped-up
the sinking.

JONTY:

Speed, fire, ice and water – not a good mix.
Any regrets?

CAPTAIN:

Of course. Many. But it was a great honour for
me to be at the helm of such a splendid ship on her
maiden voyage just as I was retiring. Her last hours
were, of course, truly dreadful and I tried to do the
best I could, despite everything.

MISH:

Is it true you were pushing the ship too fast? Had
she not been travelling flat-out, perhaps she could
have steered in time and missed the iceberg.

JONTY:

Is it true Bruce Ismay, your boss, told you he wanted you to break all the crossing records?

CAPTAIN:

That would have been irresponsible, wouldn't it?

JONTY:

You certainly broke some records – like the greatest loss of life at sea at the time.

ANDREWS:

Perhaps I can say a few words here. Captain Smith behaved heroically from the moment panic broke out on board. He managed passengers and crew calmly, without a single thought for himself. I wish to pay tribute to him.

MISH:

Mr Andrews, even though your design clearly wasn't unsinkable, survivors spoke of your own sacrifice and support in helping people scramble into lifeboats. So you really weren't the villain of the story, as some may imagine.

ANDREWS:

Thank you. I can't begin to describe how it feels to be so helpless as your own beloved creation breaks up before your eyes, with everyone in great peril. I'm not here to blame others, but I did strongly recommend she had at least 46 lifeboats, watertight bulkheads that went all the way up to B deck, and a double hull to protect the ship from collisions. I was ignored by senior management.

JONTY:

Bruce Ismay or Lord Pirrie, your uncle?

ANDREWS:

I can't possibly say. I was told more lifeboats would clutter the deck and spoil the view. We had strong arguments about that. The ship wasn't as I'd planned.

MISH:

Perhaps such thoughts were going through your mind when a steward, who was the last person to see you alive, saw you staring at a painting of Plymouth harbour in the first-class smoking room. You sat in a daze, not even wearing a lifebelt. You must have felt devastated. Did you realise what was happening?

JONTY:

Did it really sink in? Excuse my choice of words.

ANDREWS:

Of course. I assessed the situation quickly and told Captain Smith the honest and terrible truth. I can't begin to tell you how that felt.

CAPTAIN:

Mr Andrews faced the unfolding disaster with great courage, which I admired. Unfortunately, circumstances were too far out of our control.

JONTY:

I'm not so sure all the victims would look at it quite like that. Are you prepared to admit any blame, either of you?

ANDREWS:

Of course. We've both had plenty of time to reflect on all that went wrong.

CAPTAIN:

With hindsight, I shouldn't have cancelled lifeboat drill that day. I should have taken more notice of

the ice warnings. Hindsight is a wonderful thing, of course.

MISH:

Let me read this summary to you both: 'Over two-thirds of passengers and crew lost their lives in the freezing North Atlantic water when the world's largest and most luxurious passenger liner struck an iceberg just before midnight on 14th April, 1912. In response to widespread shock and public outcry, the British Government ordered an inquiry to investigate how the 'unsinkable' ship could have sunk on her maiden voyage.'

JONTY:

Yes, evidence given by survivors, ship building plans, accounts from experts, photographs and emergency telegrams helped the court conclude that the disaster was caused by 'excessive speed, insufficient lifeboat capacity, the flawed ship design, lack of organisation, poor visibility, even missing binoculars'. So how do you explain one of the greatest maritime disasters in history?

CAPTAIN:

All of the above – unforeseen circumstances and jolly bad luck.

ANDREWS:

Two words have haunted me all these years. 'If only.' I can say no more.

MISH:

Were the claims that *Titanic* was unsinkable the result of gross arrogance?

ANDREWS:

I never used the term 'unsinkable'. But yes, I think arrogance played a part.

JONTY:

On that bombshell, we move on to the rest of the story.

MISH:

Please stay with us, Captain Smith and Mr Andrews, for a more relaxed chat with other *Titanic* ghosts shortly. In the meantime, we return to the giant plasma screen to revisit the stricken ship in her final hour or so...

And the band played on

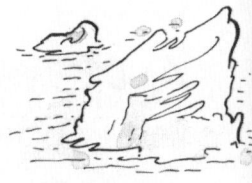

15TH APRIL 1912 — 1.30 A.M. THE RUSH FOR LIMITED LIFEBOAT SPACE CONTINUES...

OI - IT'S FOR WOMEN AND CHILDREN. ALL MEN GET OUT!

STOP ALL THIS PANIC!

OFFICER HAROLD LOWE SHOOTS A PISTOL THREE TIMES.

Ghosts reunited

MISH:

Welcome back to the *Live from the Crypt* sofa,
where we're delighted to have the ghosts of
Captain Smith and Thomas Andrews still with
us and about to meet another ghost who will be
joining us onscreen.

JONTY:

Yes, this is 'Ghosts Reunited' where we bring together ghosts who haven't met for a while, which could make for an interesting encounter. We are hoping to link up with a rather formidable lady from a cemetery in Westbury, New York. Are you there, Mrs Brown?

MOLLY:

(On screen) Indeed I am. And I've got a few words to say to that captain.

MISH:

Well, before you do, perhaps you can tell us why you were on *Titanic* in the first place and why you became a famous survivor of the disaster.

MOLLY:

That's a stupid question. I hope I haven't been disturbed just to answer a lot of twaddle. Now, where's that captain?

JONTY:

First of all, Mrs Brown, is it true you were travelling first class? I think you were a wealthy American passenger.

MOLLY:

What's that got to do with the price of kippers? Like I always say, 'It isn't who you are, nor what you have, but what you are that counts.' Now, Captain, what have you got to say for yourself?

CAPTAIN:

Ah yes, I do remember meeting you on deck, Mrs Brown. You were trying to organise people, I recall.

MOLLY:

Trying? I think you'll find I succeeded. If you'd organised the lifeboats better, I wouldn't have had to take matters into my own hands. It was utter pandemonium.

ANDREWS:

(whispering) Oh, it's her – the bossy lady with a lot to say.

MOLLY:

I heard that! I'll have you know, you could have done with people like me running that wretched ship. I would have sorted out that iceberg, too, I can tell you. No one messes with me, you know.

ANDREWS:

We wouldn't dare!

MOLLY:

As a first-class passenger, I expected a far higher standard of service. Being dumped in the ocean in the middle of the night was far from an upgrade.

MISH:

Why were you on the ship in the first place, Mrs Brown?

MOLLY:

Why do you think? I needed to get back to New York from Europe. I was on vacation with my daughter and got news my grandchild was ill back home. I got on the earliest ship, which happened to be the ghastly *Titanic*, and I told my daughter to stay in London, which it is just as well she did.

JONTY:

How did you escape the sinking ship, Mrs Brown?

MOLLY:

That's pretty obvious, isn't it, young man? I hopped

into lifeboat six. Mind you, that was after I gave that captain a piece of my mind, didn't I, Smith?

CAPTAIN:

Indeed you did, Mrs. Brown. A rather large piece at that.

MOLLY:

I believe in speaking my mind. My mind was already made-up when I was born. I'm from Missouri. As soon as I got in that lifeboat I took command. It had a few feeble men in it, so I demanded us women should take the oars.

MISH:

Is it right you were picked up by a rescue ship hours later?

MOLLY:

Of course I was, haven't you read your notes? I got to work organising the crew and everyone else to sort out the survivors and dish out food and blankets. I like to keep busy. I immediately set up the Survivors' Committee and was obviously elected Chairwoman. We raised thousands of dollars.

JONTY:

And this was even before you arrived in New York, where apparently news of your efforts had already made you famous.

MOLLY:

I don't go in for all that fame nonsense. I had work to do. No point sitting about feeling sorry for yourself, isn't that so, Captain?

CAPTAIN:

Quite right, Mrs Brown. I quite agree.

MOLLY:

You wouldn't dare disagree after all your shambles and shenanigans.

MISH:

Is it true some people called you the 'Heroine of the *Titanic*'?

MOLLY:

I couldn't stand all that sort of fuss. I've got a copy of the letter I wrote to my daughter when we docked in New York. This is what I wrote:

'After being brined, salted and pickled in mid ocean I am now high and dry... I have had flowers, letters, telegrams – until I am befuddled. They are petitioning Congress to give me a medal... If I must call a specialist to examine my head it is due to the title of Heroine of the *Titanic*.'

ANDREWS:

It was very good of you to be so considerate to other survivors, Mrs Brown.

MOLLY:

Nonsense, you silly man. It's what must be done. I then went on to promote women's rights and two years later I became the first woman to run for the US Congress. I got the *Titanic* Memorial built in Washington and continued with the Survivors Committee. You can imagine how furious I was when they wouldn't let me have my say at the *Titanic* Inquiry – just because I'm a woman!

JONTY:

I bet you had words to say about that.

MOLLY:

I did. RUDE ones. Anyway, World War I came so I got cracking on setting up a relief station for the soldiers. Can you believe they awarded me the French Legion of Honour for my work with *Titanic* survivors and for my efforts during the war? Twenty years after *Titanic* sank, I came to an end myself. They buried me here in New York with my husband.

MISH:

What you don't know, Mrs Brown, is that Hollywood got hold of your story and made you into the 'unsinkable Molly Brown'.

MOLLY:

What utter nonsense. My name is Margaret, not Molly. I think I might sue.

JONTY:

I don't think Sue Brown sounds as good as Molly Brown! See what I did there?

MISH:

Quickly moving on... just in time to turn off Mrs Brown's microphone and her rather strong words.

We'll take another look at the giant plasma screen to see just how *Titanic* is getting on. It doesn't look too good, I'm afraid...

Going down

15TH APRIL 1912 — 2.15 A.M. WITH LIFEBOATS AND FOUR COLLAPSIBLE BOATS LAUNCHED, OVER 1,500 PEOPLE ARE STILL LEFT ON BOARD.

WATER'S POURING IN THE PORTHOLES. IT'S ONLY A MATTER OF MINUTES NOW. WHAT A TOTAL NIGHTMARE.

ANYONE GOT A TORCH?

2.18 A.M. THE BAND STILL PLAYS AS ALL THE LIGHTS GO OUT.

WITH AN EAR-SPLITTING CRACK, *TITANIC* BREAKS IN TWO.

BLIMEY!

QUICK, ROW AWAY OR WE'LL GET SUCKED DOWN WITH IT.

2.20 A.M. WITH A FINAL HISS AND SIGH, THE STERN SINKS FOREVER TO THE SEABED.

SHE'S GONE.

IT'S ALL GONE DEATHLY QUIET.

WITH HUNDREDS OF PEOPLE IN THE FREEZING WATER, THE LIFEBOATS DRIFT OUT OF REACH.

IT PROBABLY TOOK 15 MINUTES FOR THE SINKING *TITANIC* TO REACH THE SEABED, DESCENDING AT A SPEED OF AROUND 17 KILOMETRES PER HOUR (10 MILES PER HOUR). THE TWO MAIN PARTS LIE ABOUT 600 METRES (1,969 FEET) APART ON THE SEABED.

Spin the news

ALEEMA:

And now it's 'Spin the News', where I spin a dial for the news headlines for a day in April 1912 *(spins a dial which stops at 16th April)*. 16th April. Newspapers that day had the breaking news of *Titanic*'s fate, but details were often sketchy or wrong at first. To review the newspapers with me tonight are two ghosts on screen in England and Scotland. Let's look at some of the front pages. Some said there were no lives lost, whilst others reported '1,500 to 1,800 dead'. It took some time before those grim numbers were fully known.

We are joined by Noël Leslie, the Countess of Rothes, from her grave at the Kirk on the Green Churchyard, Fife, in Scotland. What was it like reading those newspapers at the time?

COUNTESS:

Well, of course, we didn't. Not until days later. Gladys, my cousin, and I were lucky to escape from *Titanic* in a lifeboat and we both took the oars. Hours later we were picked up by a ship called the *Carpathia*. It was very tricky scrambling up the swaying rope ladder on the moving ocean but we managed it and helped the others. Some had to be hoisted up in large rope nets. The children were terribly scared of course, so I did my best to comfort them.

ALEEMA:

Newspapers called you 'the plucky little countess' and you were the subject of a media frenzy when you arrived in New York a few days later.

COUNTESS:

Well yes, they did go a bit overboard. It's just that the sailor in charge of lifeboat eight, Thomas Jones, told reporters that I had a lot to say for myself, which is why he put me in charge of steering our boat, then rowing and comforting the women and children who were sobbing. Thomas even presented me with the brass number eight from our lifeboat and ever since we have kept in touch every Christmas. Such a nice man.

ALEEMA:

I suppose newspaper reporters rushed to interview you as soon as possible?

COUNTESS:

All the time – and for years to come. They liked the idea of a supposedly glamorous countess travelling first class, then mucking in with all the steerage women and children. I just did what I could. I saw a lot more ghastliness when I worked as a nurse during World War I, I can tell you.

ALEEMA:

As you died in 1956, you never knew about the

films that came out about *Titanic* and that you were portrayed as something of a glitzy heroine. After all, on that date of 16th April 1912, you were on the ship *Carpathia* and courageously caring for everyone with your characteristic 'stiff upper lip'.

COUNTESS:

It wasn't glitzy, I assure you. I just got on with it. Of course, the charming ship's captain did a wonderful job of rallying us all and getting us safely to America.

ALEEMA:

I'm glad you mentioned the captain – Captain Arthur Rostron – who we hope is appearing on screen, coming to us from a cemetery in Hampshire, England.

ROSTRON:

Good evening – I've been listening to the countess with great interest, as I remember her well. She kept very busy serving hot drinks to everyone. It was literally 'all hands on deck' when we arrived at the scene of the disaster.

ALEEMA:

How did you first hear about *Titanic*'s fate?

ROSTRON:

We'd left New York four days earlier and were sailing to Europe with 740 passengers of our own. I'd heard all about the wondrous ship *Titanic*, of course, but when we picked up a radio S.O.S. message that she'd struck an iceberg and was sinking fast nearly sixty miles from us, I was flabbergasted. But there was no time to lose, so it was full steam ahead whilst we prepared our ship to take on hundreds of survivors.

ALEEMA:

So you must have been the first person in the world to hear one of the biggest news stories of all time?

ROSTRON:

I suppose so. It didn't strike me as a news story, but an emergency mission. Top speed for the *Carpathia* wasn't much more than 14 knots, so I ordered extra stokers to make more steam and accelerate the ship to over 17 knots. I even ordered a close-down in the ship's heating to divert more steam to the engines.

It was a risky move, not least because we had to dodge icebergs. Even then, it took us about three and a half hours to get there.

COUNTESS:

I can't begin to tell you how relieved we were when we caught sight of your wonderful ship on the horizon. We were all so cold and miserable. I dread to think what would have become of us if you hadn't responded so swiftly.

ALEEMA:

We'll look at the rescue mission shortly on the big screen, but just tell us how the newspapers reported your part in all this, Captain Rostron.

ROSTRON:

For some reason I got a lot of attention – a bit like the knight in shining armour dashing to the rescue in the nick of time. Of course, it was my marvellous crew that did so much of the heavy work. When we eventually returned to New York, the world's newspapers were swarming all over us. I was just pleased to be able to do my bit to help. Poor Bruce Ismay, the White Star Line boss, locked

himself away in a cabin and hardly spoke. He was a broken man.

ALEEMA:

Later on you made the front pages of newspapers yourself, Captain Rostron.

ROSTRON:

I suppose you mean awards and trophies. It seems a terrible thing to say, but *Titanic's* fate boosted my career no end. I eventually became Sir Arthur Rostron!

ALEEMA:

And we even have a news clip of you after all the official enquiries, being presented with an award by the unsinkable Mrs Brown.

COUNTESS:

Oh, her!

ROSTRON:

They also awarded me a U.S. Congressional Gold Medal.

ALEEMA:

Well, between you, Countess and Captain, you certainly made the news headlines in April 1912 and beyond. Thank you for joining us. There's just time to return to the giant plasma screen storyboard to see the *Carpathia* in action...

LAST CLIP COMING UP.

Rescue

THIS IS NO TIME FOR A WRETCHED FIREWORK DISPLAY.

WHERE'S *TITANIC*?

SUNK.

8.30 A.M. LIFEBOAT 12 IS THE LAST TO REACH THE *CARPATHIA*.

ANY CHANCE OF BREAKFAST FOR 60 MORE?

DID WE MISS ANYTHING?

WITH THE LAST SURVIVORS SCRAMBLING ABOARD THE *CARPATHIA*, THE *CALIFORNIAN* ARRIVES. IT SEARCHES THE AREA FOR SEVERAL HOURS BUT FAILS TO FIND ANY SURVIVORS.

8.50 A M — 6½ HOURS AFTER *TITANIC* SANK, THE *CARPATHIA* CARRIES AWAY THE 705 SURVIVORS.

THE *CARPATHIA* ARRIVES IN NEW YORK TO MASSIVE CROWDS ON 18TH APRIL.

CARPATHIA WILL DOCK WITH SURVIVORS TONIGHT; FACTS OF TRAGEDY BEING WITHHELD FROM WORLD

Sink or Swim

GAIL:

Welcome to 'Sink or Swim', the game show where ghosts tell us their *Titanic* tales. Each team member will try to smuggle a lie past the opposing team. If the false fact is correctly spotted by the opposite team, they win a point – but if it isn't, the first team wins the point. It could all get exciting... or not, depending on tonight's teams. Let's meet them...

IDA STRAUS:
1ST CLASS
TEAM CAPTAIN

IDA:

Hello, I'm Ida Straus and captain of the First-Class Team. We were well-known wealthy American passengers who sadly didn't make it to the lifeboats. I am joined by John Astor and Benjamin Guggenheim. As over 60% of first-class passengers survived, unlike only 24% of third-class, I guess you could say we feel a little cheated and deserve to win tonight's show.

LILLIAN ASPLUND:
3RD CLASS
TEAM CAPTAIN

LILLIAN:

Hi there, I'm Lillian Asplund and captain of the
Lower-Class Team. We're a mixed bunch and two
of us were lucky to be among the 37% of *Titanic*
passengers who survived and lived for years
afterwards – in my case, until 2006. I'm joined by
Violet and Joseph. As 75% of survivors were female,
you can probably guess which of us didn't make it.
Maybe luck is on our side tonight.

GAIL:

So now we've met tonight's teams, I shall ask Ida
to start off by telling us her *Titanic* tale, then Lillian
will confer with her team and decide which of Ida's
details is fake news that must be sunk forever. So it's
over to you, Ida.

IDA:

Well, I was on *Titanic* with my husband, Isidor
Straus, who owned Macy's department store
with his brother. Although originally Jews from
Germany, we were American citizens in our
sixties and thrilled to be travelling on *Titanic* with
its fabulous Jewish kosher kitchen, heading back
from Germany to New York. I had Ellen, my
maid, with me, and little Fritz, our pet dachshund.
We were having a lovely time until they woke
us on the Sunday night and sent us up to the
lifeboats. We were told to get in lifeboat eight but
my husband refused as the order was 'women and
children first'. I wasn't going anywhere without
him and insisted, 'where he went, I went'. I told
my maid to get in the lifeboat and passed her my
fur coat and told her I wouldn't need it anymore.

Then I passed her little Fritz to hide inside the coat and told her to look after him always. My husband and I turned away, walked along the deck as the band played, held hands and waited. A wave swept us into the sea and that was the end for both of us.

GAIL:

Thank you for your moving story, Ida. But which of those details is made-up nonsense and *Titanic* twaddle? That's for Lillian and her team to guess. I can see they are busily arguing among themselves, so what have you decided?

LILLIAN:

Hmm, this is a tricky one. It all sounds possible but why would you need a maid on a luxury ship? Maybe this Ellen wasn't real. Or maybe the lifeboat thing didn't happen and you were just too slow getting up on deck. We know that a couple of lapdogs were said to survive but... we think you'd never hand over an expensive fur coat and not want to keep warm yourself. We think the fur coat was fake.

GAIL:

Fake fur or a fake fact? Well, let's see. Ida, was your fur coat true or false?

IDA:

It was... TRUE. I did give Ellen my fur coat.

GAIL:

So what was the fib you smuggled into your story?

IDA:

The fib was Fritz. We had no dog and that bit was totally made up.

GAIL:

Well done, Ida – that's a point to the First-Class Team. So now can we have Lillian's *Titanic* Tale, from the Lower-Class Team?

LILLIAN:

To be honest, this is the first time I've spoken publicly about what happened that night, as the horrible event was something I didn't want to dwell on. My parents were Swedish and we were returning from Sweden to our home in Worcester, Massachusetts in the USA. We travelled in steerage – that's the cheapest class, as there were my parents and us five children. I was only five years old at the time. I remember clutching my teddy bear as we walked past the band and when they saw me, they began playing 'Teddy Bear's Picnic' to stop me from crying, which it did. I remember being handed down into the lowering lifeboat with my mother and brother, Felix. The sight of my father still holding my twin brother and other two brothers as we drifted away has haunted me ever since. They didn't survive. My mother, Felix and I returned to Massachusetts without them and I said no more about it, right up to my death at the age of 99. So that's my story, with an untrue bit thrown in. What was it?

GAIL:

Thank you, Lillian. Another sad story. So it's now back to Ida and her team, who are already debating fiercely. Can you pin down Lillian's piece of *Titanic* twaddle to make it sink without trace?

IDA:

We can't decide if you invented the Swedish bit, or the Massachusetts part, as you don't sound as if you come from either! Or maybe you weren't really a twin. There again, none of us have ever heard of a song called 'Teddy Bear's Picnic' so we think we'll choose that as the fib. That never happened.

GAIL:

So was the teddy bear tune bear fact or a bear-faced lie? Lillian, tell us.

LILLIAN:

It was... FALSE. I don't even remember the band. In fact, 'The Teddy Bears' Picnic' was an American tune composed the year after I was born but I wouldn't have known that as it didn't have words written for it until twenty years after *Titanic*.

GAIL:

So that means the First-Class Team now has two points and it's back to them to tell us another *Titanic* tale. It's John Astor's turn to tell us his story.

JOHN ASTOR
1ST CLASS

JOHN:

My new wife, Madeleine, and I had been on holiday to Europe and we decided to travel back home to New York, where I owned some big hotels. What better way than sailing in luxury on *Titanic*? That was our mistake. I was 47 years old and 18-year-old Madeleine was expecting our baby, so we were returning to America to ensure our child would be born a real American. Apparently, we were the wealthiest passengers onboard ship. We had Kitty with us, our darling pet Airedale dog. After the ship's collision, I was convinced it wasn't serious and that we were safer onboard than on a little lifeboat. In the end, Madeleine got into one of the boats whilst I stayed on the ship and returned to my game of cards where I was already winning several hundred dollars. Before long, all the lifeboats had gone and the ship went down with me on it. They found my body, with my initials on my shirt collar. There was money in my pockets: £225 and $2,440. A shame I never got to spend it.

GAIL:

Thank you, John Jacob Astor IV for your *Titanic* Tale, packed with little bits of detail, but which of them is total balderdash? Over to Lillian to decide.

LILLIAN:

It all sounds so likely and I certainly know you were a multi-millionaire. We're not sure about the young age of your wife or all that cash in your pockets. Why would you need that on a ship? There again, who calls a dog 'Kitty'? Yes, we think you made up the bit about a pet dog.

GAIL:

So is this another shaggy dog story with an imaginary pet? Time to tell if Kitty was true or false.

JOHN:

It was... TRUE. We did have an Airedale on board called Kitty, who sadly perished like I did.

GAIL:

So what was the splash of hogwash that you dribbled into your account, John?

JOHN:

I did not return casually to my gambling game of cards as the ship was sinking.

GAIL:

We're glad to hear it. There is a legend that claims that after the ship hit the iceberg you said to the barman 'I know I asked for ice, but this is ridiculous!' True?

JOHN:

I couldn't possibly comment.

VIOLET JESSOP:
STAFF

GAIL:

Nonetheless, your team wins yet another point. Let's see if the lower classes can score in the next *Titanic* tale told to us by Violet Jessop. Over to you, Violet.

VIOLET:

I was a 24-year-old nurse and stewardess for the White Star Line and joined the *Titanic* in Southampton. The staff were delighted with our quarters and I often saw Thomas Andrews, the ship's designer. He always stopped to chat cheerfully and was looking forward to getting back home to Ireland, which is where I came from, too. That night I was in my bunk when we hit the iceberg. I was ordered on deck to act calmly and explain to the non-English speakers who struggled to follow the instructions being given. I watched as the crew loaded the lifeboats and was ordered into lifeboat 16. As the boat was lowered into the sea, an officer gave me a baby to look after. When we were on board the *Carpathia* rescue ship, a woman grabbed the baby from me and ran off. I presumed she was the mother. Years later, in 1950, I received a telephone call asking me if I'd saved a baby on the night *Titanic* sank. I said I had but I had never mentioned it to anyone. Then the voice said, 'I was that baby and I'm now a movie actor and I'd like to meet you in Hollywood as we're making a movie about *Titanic*.' It was called *A Night to Remember.*

GAIL:

Thanks to Violet for an interesting account, but which part was complete nonsense? It's now up to Ida's team to decide.

IDA:

Ooh, any of that could be complete poppycock. There again, it all had a ring of truth. I don't remember an Irish stewardess called Violet, but I guess you could have been working quietly away in the background. We think you made up all that about rescuing a baby and having it snatched away. That's a lie.

GAIL:

Very well, let's ask Violet if she really did carry a stranger's baby, only to have it snatched from her later. True or false?

VIOLET:

It was... TRUE. It all happened like I said and I even got a phone call many years later from someone who said, 'I was that baby' but they hung up and I never met them. So all that movie stuff was a lie – although I did go to watch *A Night to Remember* about *Titanic*, which was released in 1958.

GAIL:

Well done, Violet – that means your team has scored a point at last. Let's see if you can spot a lie from Benjamin Guggenheim and increase your score...

BENJAMIN
GUGGENHEIM:
1ST CLASS

BENJAMIN:

I guess you could call me a successful 46-year-old American businessman and part of the great Jewish community on board. With Victor, my valet, I was having a swell time on the ship until what I thought was just a little bump. In fact, I remember saying that the scrape will need only a little repair and 'tomorrow *Titanic* will go on again'. Having purchased a major painting by the artist Renoir in France, I was taking it home to our

Guggenheim Museum in New York. I was more concerned about the painting when the ship started sinking. When I realised it was hopeless, Victor and I changed into our evening wear and I said we would 'go down with the ship like gentlemen'. I gave a message to someone on a lifeboat, which told my wife 'I've done my best in doing my duty'. Then Victor and I sat on deckchairs in the foyer of the Grand Staircase, sipping brandy and smoking cigars as we went down with the ship. And that was all there was to it.

GAIL:

What a vivid picture you painted, Benjamin – but which part of it was pure fantasy? Can Lillian's team spot the rot? Over to the Lower Classes...

LILLIAN:

I'm not sure if we all agree. I can't think you would coolly sit back in your best clothes with your expensive masterpiece painting below decks without trying to rescue it. We seem to think the Guggenheim Museum opened years later, anyway. So we think you invented the Renoir painting story.

GAIL:

In that case, let's ask Benjamin if his French masterpiece was just a figment of his imagination. True or false?

BENJAMIN:

It was... FALSE. There was no such masterpiece among my luggage but the rest was all true.

GAIL:

The score is now 3 points to First-Class and 2 points to Lower-Class. Maybe it will end in a draw after we hear the final *Titanic* tale. Over to you, Joseph.

JOSEPH:

My full name is Joseph Philippe Lemercier Laroche. As far as I know, I was one of only three Afro-Caribbean passengers on *Titanic*. I was born in Haiti and, as my father was French, I was sent to school in France, where I trained as an engineer. I was 25 years old and had two little daughters. Juliette, my wife, was expecting our third child so we decided to go back to Haiti for the birth and to be with my parents. It was my mother who sent us tickets to sail on a ship called *La France*.

We then found its rules banned children from dining with their parents in the dining room, so I managed to exchange our tickets for second-class tickets on *Titanic*, where we actually dined in the same dining room as the first-class passengers. One evening we were even invited to the captain's table where I also discussed engineering with the ship's designer, Mr Andrews. As the ship was sinking, I took my wife and children up to the boat deck. I wrapped my coat around her and said, 'Here, take this, you are going to need it. I'll get another boat. God be with you. I'll see you in New York.' Alas, I never did, as I went down with the ship. If only we hadn't swapped ships in the beginning, eh?

GAIL:

That account from Joseph has certainly given the First-Class Team plenty to think about and I can see them discussing it intently. What is your verdict, Ida?

IDA:

We're all in complete agreement about the false part of the story. In fact, we all remember seeing Joseph and his family in the first-class dining room

JOSEPH LEMERCIER:
2ND CLASS

and seeing heads turn. Some people were horrified
that second-class passengers should be allowed
anywhere near us. Had the captain dined with
him, it would have caused almost as much of a
disturbance as the iceberg. Such a thing would never
be allowed so that bit is definitely a lie.

GAIL:

You certainly seem to be sure and united, so we had better ask Joseph to tell us if he really did dine at Captain Smith's table. True or false?

JOSEPH:

It was... FALSE. You're quite right, we never did dine with the captain.

GAIL:

In that case, it only remains for me to give the final score. The First-Class Team has 4 points and the Lower-Class Team has 2 points – so our winners are the First-Class Passengers, who have the lion's share and the upper hand.

LILLIAN:

As they always do. The lower-classes have always had to make-do with less!

GAIL:

Well that's certainly a thought to finish on. Thank you to both teams, for telling us your own true stories with a few whopping lies thrown in. We have managed to sink the *Titanic* twaddle and let the truth swim to the surface. That's all from us here, as I hand you back to Mish and Jonty on the studio sofa. Goodnight.

Wreck-emendations

MISH:

You join us back on the *Live from the Crypt* sofa, where our two ghostly guests have been listening to everything with great interest. Any thoughts, I wonder?

CAPTAIN:

We have met some of the last guests, as they rest with us down here in the wreck.

ANDREWS:

The wreck is full of many watery ghosts, of course.

JONTY:

We thought you might wreck-ognise some of them. See what I did there?

MISH:

No more jokes, Jonty. Moving on...

JONTY:

I guess we can't blame our two guests for being WRECKLESS up here, can we?

CAPTAIN:

I think it's time we left. *(stands)*

ANDREWS:

I agree. We'll return to our resting place, if you don't mind.

JONTY:

When you get there, will you WRECK-ognise it?

MISH:

No, Jonty. Please, before you go, would you like to say something for the record?

JONTY:

Don't you mean WRECK-ord?

CAPTAIN:

Right, that's it...

ANDREWS:

Goodnight.
(They leave... SPLASH!)

JONTY:

Was it something I said?

MISH:

Yes. What a shame they didn't stay to see these two video clips from their ghost daughters. First up is Helen Melville Russell-Cooke, the daughter of Captain Smith, who is talking to us from Brookwood Cemetery in Surrey, England.

HELEN:

Hello – I just want to say how daddy was cleared of blame in the inquiries into the *Titanic* disaster. In fact, he was praised by many for his bravery and courage. The only person criticised by both enquiries was the captain of the *Californian*, the ship that stood by just a few miles off, its crew watching the emergency flares being fired by *Titanic*, without doing anything about it until it was too late. My father always remained a hero to me and my family.

JONTY:

I'm sure the captain would welcome those words from his own daughter.

MISH:

And the next message is from Elizabeth, the daughter of Thomas Andrews, whom he called 'Elba'. Although only a baby when her father sank with *Titanic*, Elba grew up to become the first woman to get a pilot's licence in Northern Ireland. She joins us from a churchyard near Belfast...

ELBA:

Hello – I want to say how proud I am of my
father. His ship design was amazing and no one
could have foreseen such a catastrophic collision
with rock-hard jagged ice. He'd argued for more
lifeboats and thankfully, after the disaster, the
rules were changed so that all ships have to
carry enough lifeboats for the number of people
on board. So many survivors called my father
a hero for saving them as the ship went down.
If only he had lived to see my achievements
and his brother becoming prime minister of
Northern Ireland.

JONTY:

With thanks to Elba Andrews there. At least it's
good to know some lessons were learned from
the 1,500 lives lost on *Titanic*. Increased training
and better emergency equipment and procedures
have greatly improved safety on ships and
saved many lives since. You could even say the
fate of *Titanic* brought about many WRECK-
emendations. See what I did there?

MISH:

How about moving on, Jonty? I think it's about time we close *Live from the Crypt* until another time. Maybe we'll return before the wreck finally breaks up.

JONTY:

They say it will crumble away down there within a few more years.

MISH:

If you watch the 1997 film *Titanic*, you'll see at the start just how amazing the wreck down there looks.

JONTY:

I much prefer that sci-fi movie where a gigantic magic submarine rises from the depths of the ocean and rescues hundreds of drowning people from the icy waves then carries them safely back to Britain where they all wave cheerfully.

MISH:

What's the film called?

JONTY:

It's a weird title – 'Cinatit'.

MISH:

Jonty – you were watching *Titanic* backwards.

JONTY:

Really? Well at least it had a happy ending.

MISH:

Doh! Talking of happy endings, we'd better go before you upset anyone else. So it just remains for us to say... from Jonty Yardley and me, Mish Varma...

BOTH:

Goodnight!
(End Music & Credits)

N.B. The exact number of people on *Titanic* was not known, but the official total of all passengers and crew is 2,229. The number of survivors varies from 701–713.

Total Passengers = 1,316 (498 survived)
Total Crew   = 913 (215 survived)
Total on *Titanic* = 2,229
Total survivors   = 713

Only 340 bodies were recovered. 150 were buried in Fairview Lawn Cemetery, Halifax, Canada (just half of them identified).

Family tree
of Captain Smith

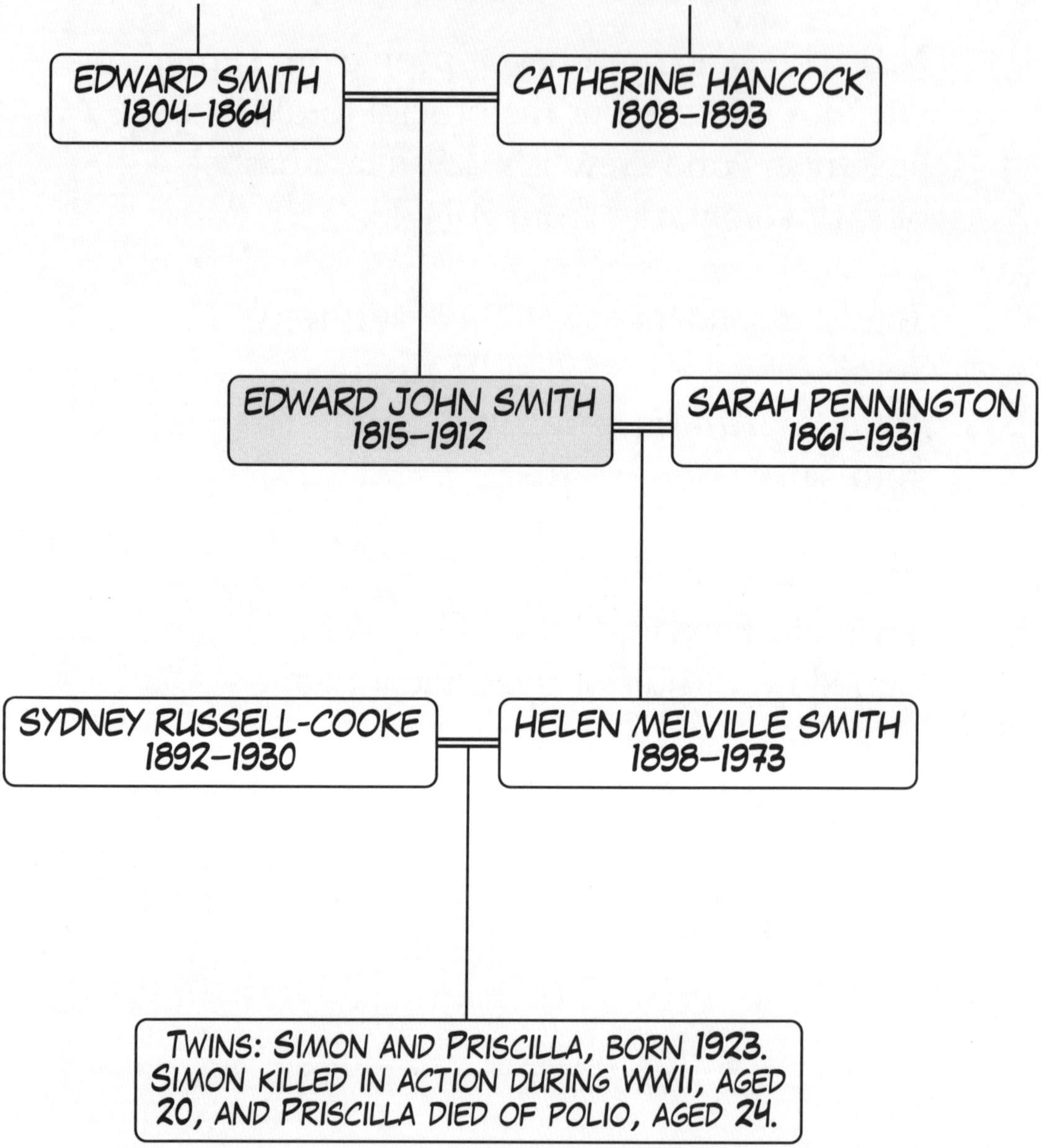

EDWARD SMITH 1804–1864	CATHERINE HANCOCK 1808–1893

EDWARD JOHN SMITH 1815–1912	SARAH PENNINGTON 1861–1931

SYDNEY RUSSELL-COOKE 1892–1930	HELEN MELVILLE SMITH 1898–1973

TWINS: SIMON AND PRISCILLA, BORN 1923. SIMON KILLED IN ACTION DURING WWII, AGED 20, AND PRISCILLA DIED OF POLIO, AGED 24.

Timeline

1907
Lord Pirrie of Harland & Wolff shipbuilders and Bruce Ismay of The White Star Line meet to plan building immense luxury passenger ships.

31ST MARCH 1909
Construction of *Titanic* begins at Harland & Wolff's shipyard in Belfast.

31ST MAY 1911

Titanic is lathered with soap and pushed into the water for fitting-out.

2ND APRIL 1912

Titanic leaves dock for sea trials, then heads to Southampton, England.

3RD–10TH APRIL 1912

Titanic is loaded with supplies and her crew is hired.

10TH APRIL 1912

9:30–11:30 a.m. passengers board the ship. At noon, *Titanic* leaves for her maiden voyage. First stop is in Cherbourg, France – arriving 6:30 p.m. and leaving at 8:10 p.m. for Queenstown, Ireland (now known as Cobh).

11TH APRIL 1912

1:30 p.m. *Titanic* leaves Queenstown and heads across the Atlantic for New York. Passengers enjoy life on the luxurious ship.

14TH APRIL 1912 9:20 P.M.

Weather fine. Captain Smith retires to his room.

9:40 P.M.

The last of several warnings about icebergs is received in the wireless room. This warning never makes it to the bridge.

11:40 P.M.

Lookouts spot an iceberg directly in front of *Titanic*. First, Officer Murdoch orders a hard turn, but *Titanic*'s starboard (right) side scrapes the iceberg. 37 seconds passed between the sighting of the iceberg and hitting it.

15TH APRIL 1912 12:05 A.M.

Captain Smith orders the crew to prepare the lifeboats and to get all passengers and crew up on deck.

12:45 A.M.

The first lifeboat is lowered into the freezing water.

2:18 A.M.

Titanic breaks in two.

2:20 A.M.

Titanic sinks. Over 1,500 people die.

4:10 A.M.

The *Carpathia* picks up the first of the survivors.

8:30 A.M.

The *Carpathia* picks up survivors from the last lifeboat.

18TH APRIL 1912

The *Carpathia* arrives in New York with over 700 survivors.

19TH APRIL–JULY 1912

Hearings and inquiries into the disaster are held in both the United States and Britain.

SEPTEMBER 1985

An expedition team discovers the wreck of the *Titanic* deep in the North Atlantic.

1997

The epic film *Titanic* is released to great publicity. It is the most expensive film ever made at the time, with a production budget of $200 million (more than it cost to build the ship!). *Titanic* is the first film to earn over a billion dollars at the global box office, remaining the highest-grossing film ever for several years.

2012

Centenary of the *Titanic* disaster, when Australian businessman Clive Palmer announces a project to construct a replica ship of *Titanic*. Building is delayed.

Who wants to be a Titanic-heir?
(with a chance to inherit a souvenir from the Titanic)

Can you answer all the questions to win one million *Titanic* Euros?

(You can play this quiz on your own or with a contestant, a question host and an audience.)

Interviews with the Ghosts of the Titanic

1. For €100 – Who was the captain of the *Titanic*?
a) Nelson
b) Edward Smith
c) Blackbeard
d) Captain Birdseye

2. For €200 – When was *Titanic*'s maiden voyage?
a) 1910
b) 1912
c) 1914
d) 1920

3. For €300 – What did *Titanic* hit underwater?
a) A sea monster
b) A submarine
c) Rocks
d) Ice

4. For €500 – Who designed *Titanic*?
a) Nick Titan
b) Andrew Thomas
c) Thomas Andrews
d) Boaty McBoatface

5. For €1,000 – Where is the wreck of *Titanic*?
a) The North Sea
b) The North Atlantic Ocean
c) The Mariana Trench
d) Disney World

6. For €2,000 – *Titanic* belonged to which shipping line?
a) Black Star Line
b) Blue Moon Line
c) Red Flag Line
d) White Star Line

7. For €4,000 – Which shipbuilder built *Titanic*?
a) Harland & Wolff, Belfast
b) Cammell Laird, Liverpool
c) Cunard Company, Southampton
d) Lawrence & Foulkes, New York

8. For €8,000 – What did RMS stand for?
a) Royal Mail Ship
b) Regular Maritime Service
c) Russian Military Ship
d) Royal Merchant Steamer

9. For €16,000 – At what time did *Titanic* strike the iceberg?
a) 19.12
b) 20.32
c) 23.40
d) 23.55

10. For €32,000 – Why didn't *Titanic* have more than
    twenty lifeboats?
a) 'Twenty is plenty' was the slogan
b) More would spoil the view
c) More would make the ship too heavy
d) They forgot to load any more

11. For €64,000 – Who was called 'The Heroine of *Titanic*'?
a) Lady Duff Gordon
b) Ida Straus
c) Violet Jessop
d) Margaret Brown

12. For €125,000 – When did the *Titanic* sink completely?
a) 02.20 on 14th April
b) 03.30 on 14th April
c) 01.15 on 15th April
d) 02.20 on 15th April

13. For €250,000 – Who was highly praised for rescuing *Titanic* survivors?
a) Bruce Ismay
b) Lord Pirrie
c) Arthur Rostron
d) Gladys Cherry

14. For €500,000 – Which ship arrived too late on the scene and was criticised in the inquiry?
a) The *Carpathia*
b) The *Caledonian*
c) The *Colorado*
d) The *Californian*

15. For 1 million – When did *Titanic*'s survivors finally arrive in New York?
a) Tuesday 18th April
b) Wednesday 18th April
c) Thursday 18th April
d) Friday 18th April

ANSWERS:
1 (B) 2 (B) 3 (D) 4 (C) 5 (B)
6 (D) 7 (A) 8 (A) 9 (C) 10 (B) 11 (D)
12 (D) 13 (C) 14 (D) 15 (C)

The points you win entitle you to this ticket:

Launch
OF
White Star Royal Mail
Triple-Screw Steamer
'TITANIC'

At Belfast,
Wednesday, 31st May, 1911, at 12.15 p.m.
Admit Bearer

'Striking the water was like a thousand knives being driven into one's body. The temperature was 28 degrees, four degrees below freezing.' Charles Lightoller, *Titanic* Second Officer (the most senior member of the crew to survive the disaster).

Glossary

BOW
Front of ship (stern = rear).

BULKHEAD
A dividing wall or barrier between separate compartments inside a ship.

BUOYANCY
The upward force on a ship that keeps it afloat if watertight.

KNOT
One nautical mile (1.852 km) per hour.

KOSHER
Selling or serving food that is fit, according to Jewish law.

MAIDEN VOYAGE
The first full journey of a ship after delivery to its owners.

PORT
The left side of a ship when looking forward.

SOS
An international radio code distress signal calling for help.

STARBOARD
The right side of a ship when looking forward.

STEERAGE
The section in a passenger ship for passengers paying the lowest fares.

In the classroom

10 TITLES IN CHRONOLOGICAL ORDER:

TUTANKHAMUN
ANCIENT EGYPT AND HOWARD CARTER'S 1922 DISCOVERIES.

QIN SHI HUANG
ANCIENT CHINA AND THE TERRACOTTA ARMY DISCOVERY OF 1974.

ROMAN EMPERORS
ANCIENT ROME AND THE FIRST 5 NOTORIOUS EMPERORS AFTER JULIUS CAESAR.

HENRY VIII
TUDOR ENGLAND AND THE TURBULENT TRIALS OF KING AND COUNTRY.

PIRATES
17TH & 18TH CENTURY SWASHBUCKLING ON THE HIGH SEAS AND THE CARIBBEAN.

QUEEN VICTORIA
THE LIFE AND TIMES OF AN ENIGMATIC QUEEN AND HER VICTORIAN WORLD.

LOUIS PASTEUR
THE AGE OF SCIENTIFIC DISCOVERY: DISEASE, GERM THEORY AND HYGIENE.

SPARKY INVENTORS
THE AGE OF ELECTRICITY PIONEERS; FROM THOMAS EDISON TO NIKOLA TESLA.

WOMEN DOCTORS AND MEDICAL PIONEERS
MARIE CURIE AND THE FIRST WOMEN NOBEL PRIZE-WINNERS.

TITANIC
THE FAMOUS TRAGEDY TOLD BY THOSE WHO WERE THERE.

(ARRANGING THE BOOKS IN ORDER COULD BE AN ACTIVITY IN ITSELF!)

Each of these books is primarily for solitary reading, but they have also been designed with the option for groups to read and perform together as a play at school, home or anywhere else.

A whole class can be included, or smaller groups if individuals take on several parts. There are plenty of flexible possibilities to involve as many or as few as required.

The books can be broken up into their various scenes for reading, performing or recording on video or audio equipment separately, simultaneously or with everyone together. On the other hand, one solitary individual could, with different voices, record scenes alone. The ultimate aim is that all who read or perform should be entertained, informed, engaged and encouraged to enjoy plenty of imaginative factual fun.

Ideas for performance

As well as the 20 or so character parts in each book, there is plenty of scope for extra roles for both performers and creators behind the scenes.

Potential extra roles

FACT-CHECKER(S)

Throughout the script, various bizarre facts with unusual information appear. Occasionally a flag/banner could pop up saying 'That's TRUE!' (Maybe with an added comment such as 'Yes, they really did eat x'.) Someone could verify such facts or add an extra detail, then be responsible for holding up the sign at the appropriate time in the show.

CONTESTANTS

A few willing volunteers to sit the final quiz could swot up on information before sitting in the hotseat. If a contestant chooses the wrong answer, a replacement volunteer can take over from where they left off. Four lifelines are available: 50-50 (2 wrong answers removed), ask the host, ask the audience and ask a friend.

DIRECTOR

A suitable person will need to take control of fitting everything together, making decisions and directing the cast (as well as taking the blame!).

SOUND EFFECTS

Someone could be responsible for recording/playing appropriate sound effects, TV jingles and songs/music between scenes or to link sections. Anyone so inspired and skilled could adapt the comic strip sequences for PowerPoint (or some such) visual presentation for showing on screen.

QUIZ HOST

The questioner can read out each question followed by the four possible answers, or a PowerPoint slide can be prepared for showing each question. A second slide can also be prepared with two wrong answers omitted, should the contestant ask for the 50-50 option. The questioner shouldn't see the answer until the contestant says 'final answer', particularly if the 'ask the host' lifeline has been chosen. If the 'ask the audience' lifeline is chosen, the host asks everyone to vote for each answer in turn by raising a hand (voting only once!). After counting the votes for each question, the host repeats the figures to the contestant. If the 'ask a friend' lifeline is used, the contestant will already have chosen someone in the audience to ask. The host invites the friend to give an answer, checks if they are correct and announces the result.

Additional activities

CHARACTER CARDS

All the characters in the book (whether a genuine historical character or from the TV team) can be summarised on a card with simple headings, scores and personality characteristics. These can then be discussed, displayed or even 'played' if players compare their cards or devise 'Top Trump'-style activities. Lists of character traits/ adjectives can be added, with students having to justify why they have chosen their descriptions. Some examples follow:

CHARACTER CARD	
NAME:	

DATES:　　　**COUNTRY:**

STRENGTH	
WEAKNESS	
SKILL	
BIG MOMENT	
QUOTE	

CALM	SILLY	GRUMPY	ANGRY
CHALLENGING	CHEERFUL	POMPOUS	CLUMSY
CONFIDENT	MISERABLE	TENSE	DULL
GOOD-NATURED	CAPABLE	NERVOUS	LAZY
WISE	CHARMING	SELFISH	SHY
DREAMY	ENTHUSIASTIC	CARING	SCARY
STUBBORN	KIND	CLEVER	LIVELY
ANXIOUS	WITTY	FRIENDLY	PATIENT
CRUEL	INTENSE	SENSITIVE	SLEEPY
GLOOMY	TOUGH	ARGUMENTATIVE	GIGGLY
MOODY	DOMINEERING	SARCASTIC	BORED

TIMELINE TEASER

This could be a puzzle for individuals/pairs or a timed group competition. It would feature the timeline at the back of the book. A photocopy with a few blanks, together with a choice of answers displayed elsewhere, should keep everyone happily amused, engaged and even enraged! This offers a great way of consolidating understanding of the context of the events in the book.

MATCH THE MEANING

Chopping up a copy of the glossary provides a fun way for students to match words with their definitions, helping to learn key vocabulary and ideas.

COMMERCIAL BREAK

How about developing the advertisements from the commercial break with extra jingles, cheesy ad-talk, dialogue, sketches, slogans and even a few puppets thrown in the mix?

Index